BLACK LEGACY PRESS™

WWW.BLACKLEGACYPRESS.ORG

Negro life in New York's Harlem
A lively picture of a popular and interesting section
By
Wallace Thurman

ISBN: 978-1-63652-288-3

NEGRO LIFE IN NEW YORK'S HARLEM

A LIVELY PICTURE OF A POPULAR AND INTERESTING
SECTION

WALLACE THURMAN

TABLE OF CONTENTS

I
A LIVELY PICTURE
OF A POPULAR AND
INTERESTING SECTION

WALLACE THURMAN

Harlem has been called the Mecca of the New Negro, the center of black America's cultural renaissance, Nigger Heaven, Pickaninny Paradise, Capitol of Black America, and various other things. It has been surveyed and interpreted, explored and exploited. It has had its day in literature, in the drama, even in the tabloid press. It is considered the most popular and interesting section of contemporary New York. Its fame is international; its personality individual and inimitable. There is no Negro settlement anywhere comparable to Harlem, just as there is no other metropolis comparable to New York. As the great south side black belt of Chicago spreads and smells with the same industrial clumsiness and stockyardish vigor of Chicago, so does the black belt of New York teem and rhyme with the cosmopolitan cross currents of the world's greatest city. Harlem is Harlem because it is part and parcel of greater New York. Its rhythms are the lackadaisical rhythms of a transplanted minority group caught up and rendered half mad by the more speedy rhythms of the subway, Fifth Avenue and the Great White Way.

Negro Harlem is located on one of the choice sites of Manhattan Island. It covers the greater portion of the northwestern end, and is more free from grime, smoke and oceanic dampness than the lower eastside where most of the hyphenated American groups live. Harlem is

1

a great black city. There are no shanty-filled, mean streets. No antiquated cobble-stoned pavement; no flimsy frame fire-traps. Little Africa has fortressed itself behind brick and stone on wide important streets where the air is plentiful and sunshine can be appreciated.

There are six main north and south thoroughfares streaming through Negro Harlem—Fifth Avenue, Lenox Avenue, Seventh Avenue, Eighth Avenue, Edgecombe and St. Nicholas. Fifth Avenue begins prosperously at 125th Street, becomes a slum district above 131st Street, and finally slithers off into a warehouse-lined, dingy alleyway above 139th Street. The people seen on Fifth Avenue are either sad or nasty looking. The women seem to be drudges or drunkards, the men pugnacious and loud—petty thieves and vicious parasites. The children are pitiful specimens of ugliness and dirt.

The tenement houses in this vicinity are darkened dungheaps, festering with poverty-stricken and crime-ridden step-children of nature. This is the edge of Harlem's slum district; Fifth Avenue is its board-walk. Push carts line the curbstone, dirty push carts manned by dirtier hucksters, selling fly-specked vegetables and other cheap commodities. Evil faces leer at you from doorways and windows. Brutish men elbow you out of their way, dreary looking women scowl at and curse children playing on the sidewalk. That is Harlem's Fifth Avenue.

Lenox Avenue knows the rumble of the subway and the rattle of the crosstown street car. It is always crowded, crowded with pedestrians seeking the subway or the street car, crowded with idlers from the many pool halls and dives along its line of march, crowded with men and women from the slum district which it borders on the west and Fifth Avenue borders on the east. Lenox Avenue is Harlem's Bowery. It is dirty and noisy, its buildings ill-used, and made shaky by the subway underneath. At 140th Street it makes its one bid for respectability. On one corner there is Tabb's Restaurant and Grill, one of Harlem's most delightful and respectable eating houses; across the street is the Savoy building, housing a first-class dance hall, a motion picture theater and many small business establishments behind its stucco front. But above 141st Street Lenox Avenue gets mean and squalid, deprived of even its crowds of people, and finally peters out into a dirt pile, before leading to a car-barn at 147th St.

Seventh Avenue—Black Broadway—Harlem's main street, a place to promenade, a place to loiter, an avenue spacious and sleek with wide pavement, modern well-kept buildings, theaters, drug stores and other businesses. Seventh Avenue, down which no Negro dared walk twenty years ago unless he was prepared to fight belligerent Irishmen. Seventh Avenue, teeming with life and ablaze with color, the most interesting and important street in one of the most interesting and important city sections of greater New York.

Negro Harlem is best represented by Seventh Avenue. It is not, like Fifth Avenue, filthy and stark, nor like Lenox, squalid and dirty. It is a grand thoroughfare into which every element of Harlem population ventures either for reasons of pleasure or of business. From 125th Street to 145th Street, Seventh Avenue is a stream of dark people going to churches, theaters, restaurants, billiard halls, business offices, food markets, barber shops and apartment houses. Seventh Avenue is majestic yet warm, and it reflects both the sordid chaos and the rhythmic splendor of Harlem.

From five o'clock in the evening until way past midnight, Seventh Avenue is one electric-lit line of brilliance and activity, especially during the spring, summer and early fall months. Dwelling houses are close, overcrowded and dark. Seventh Avenue is the place to seek relief. People everywhere. Lines of people in front of the box offices of the Lafayette Theater at 132d Street, the Renaissance motion picture theater at 138th Street and the Roosevelt Theater at 145th Street. Knots of people in front of the Metropolitan Baptist Church at 129th Street and Salem M. E. Church, which dominates the corner at 129th Street.

People going into the cabarets. People going into speak-easies and saloons. Groups of boisterous men and boys, congregated on corners and in the middle of the blocks, making remarks about individuals in the passing parade. Adolescent boys and girls flaunting their youth. Street speakers on every corner. A Hindoo faker here, a loud-voiced Socialist there, a medicine doctor ballyhooing, a corn doctor, a blind musician, serious people, gay people, philanderers and preachers. Seventh Avenue is filled with deep rhythmic laughter. It is a civilized lane with primitive traits, Harlem's most representative street.

Eighth Avenue supports the elevated lines. It is noticeably negroid only from 135th Street to 145th Street. It is packed with dingy, cheap shops owned by Jews. Above 139th Street the curbstone is lined with push-cart merchants selling everything from underwear to foodstuffs. Eighth Avenue is dark and noisy. The elevated trestle and its shadows dominate the street. Few people linger along its sidewalks. Eighth Avenue is a street for business, a street for people who live west of it to cross hurriedly in order to reach places located east of it.

Edgecombe, Brandhurst and St. Nicholas Avenues are strictly residential thoroughfares of the better variety. Expensive modern apartment houses line these streets. They were once occupied by well-to-do white people who now live on Riverside Drive, West End Avenue and in Washington Heights. They are luxuriously appointed with imposing entrances, elevator service, disappearing garbage cans, and all the other appurtenances that make a modern apartment house convenient. The Negroes who live in these places are either high-salaried workingmen or professional folk.

Most of the cross streets in Harlem, lying between the main north and south thoroughfares, are monotonous and overcrowded. There is little difference between any of them save that some are more dirty and more squalid than others. They are lined with ordinary, undistinguished tenement and apartment houses. Some are well kept, others are run down. There are only four streets that are noticeably different, 136th Street, 137th Street, 138th Street and 139th Street west of Seventh Avenue and these are the only blocks in Harlem that can boast of having shade trees. An improvement association organized by people living in these streets, strives to keep them looking respectable.

Between Seventh and Eighth Avenues, is 139th Street, known among Harlemites as "strivers' row." It is the most aristocratic street in Harlem. Stanford White designed the houses for a wealthy white clientele. Moneyed Negroes now own and inhabit them. When one lives on "strivers' row" one has supposedly arrived. Harry Wills resides there, as do a number of the leading Babbitts and professional folk of Harlem.

II
200,000 NEGROES
IN HARLEM

There are approximately 200,000 Negroes in Harlem. Two hundred thousand Negroes drawn from all sections of America, from Europe, the West Indies, Africa, Asia, or where you will. Two hundred thousand Negroes living, loving, laughing, crying, procreating and dying in the segregated city section of Greater New York, about twenty-five blocks long and seven blocks wide. Like all of New York, Harlem is overcrowded. There are as many as 5,000 persons living in some single blocks; living in dark, mephitic tenements, jammed together, brownstone fronts, dingy elevator flats and modern apartment houses.

Living conditions are ribald and ridiculous. Rents are high and sleeping quarters at a premium. Landlords profiteer and accept bribes, putting out one tenant in order to house another willing to pay more rent. Tenants, in turn, sublet and profiteer on roomers. People rent a five-room apartment, originally planned for a small family, and crowd two over-sized families into it. Others lease or buy a private house and partition off spacious front and back rooms into two or three parts. Hallways are curtained off and lined with cots. Living rooms become triplex apartments. Clothes closets and washrooms become kitchenettes. Dining rooms, parlors, libraries, drawing rooms are all profaned by cots, day beds and snoring sleepers.

There is little privacy, little unused space. The man in the front room of a railroad flat, so called because each room opens into the other like coaches on a train, must pass through three other bedrooms in order to reach the bathroom stuck on the end of the kitchen. He who works nights will sleep by day in the bed of one who works days, and vice versa. Mother and father sleep in a three-quarter bed. Two adolescent children sleep on a portable cot set up in the parents' bedroom. Other cots are dragged by night from closets and corners to be set up in the dining room, in the parlor, or even in the kitchen to accommodate the remaining members of the family. It is all disconcerting, mad. There must be expansion. There is expansion, but it is not rapid enough or continuous enough to keep pace with the ever-growing population of Negro Harlem.

The first place in New York where Negroes had a segregated community was in Greenwich Village, but as the years passed and their numbers increased they soon moved northward into the twenties and lower thirties west of Sixth Avenue until they finally made one big jump and centered around west Fifty-third Street. About 1900, looking for better housing conditions, a few Negroes moved to Harlem. The Lenox Avenue subway had not yet been built and white landlords were having difficulty in keeping white tenants east of Seventh Avenue because of the poor transportation facilities. Being good businessmen they eagerly accepted the suggestion of a Negro real estate agent that these properties be opened to colored tenants. Then it was discovered that the few houses available would not be sufficient to accommodate the sudden influx. Negroes began to creep west of Lenox Avenue. White property owners and residents began to protest and tried to find means of checking or evicting unwelcome black neighbors. Negroes kept pouring in. Negro capital, belligerently organized, began to buy all available properties.

Then, to quote James Johnson, "the whole movement, in the eyes of the whites, took on the aspect of an 'invasion'; they became panic stricken and began fleeing as from a plague. The presence of one colored family in a block, no matter how well-bred and orderly, was sufficient to precipitate a flight. House after house and block after block was actually deserted. It was a great demonstration of human beings running amuck. None of them stopped to reason why they were doing it or what would happen if they didn't. The banks and the lending companies holding mortgages on these deserted houses were compelled to take them over. For some time they held these houses vacant, preferring to do that and carry the charges than to rent or sell them to colored people. But values dropped and continued to drop until at the outbreak of the war in Europe property in the northern part of Harlem had reached the nadir."

With the war came a critical shortage of common labor and the introducing of thousands of southern Negroes into northern industrial and civic centers. A great migration took place. Negroes were in search of a holy grail. Southern Negroes, tired of moral and financial blue days, struck out for the promised land, to seek adventure among factories, subways and skyscrapers. New York, of course, has always been a magnet for ambitious and adventurous Americans and foreigners. New York to the Negro meant Harlem, and the great influx included not only thousands of Negroes from every state in the Union, but also over thirty thousand immigrants from the West Indian Islands and the Caribbean regions. Harlem was the promised land.

Thanks to New York's many and varied industries, Harlem Negroes have been able to demand and find much work. There is a welcome and profitable diversity of employment. Unlike Negroes in Chicago, or in Pittsburgh, or in Detroit, no one industry is called upon to employ the greater part of their population. Negroes have made money in New York; Negroes have brought money to New York with them, and with this money they have bought property, built certain civic institutions and increased their business activities until their real estate holdings are now valued at more than sixty million dollars.

III
THE SOCIAL LIFE
OF HARLEM

The social life of Harlem is both complex and diversified. Here you have two hundred thousand people collectively known as Negroes. You have pure-blooded Africans, British Negroes, Spanish Negroes, Portuguese Negroes, Dutch Negroes, Danish Negroes, Cubans, Porto Ricans, Arabians, East Indians and black Abyssinian Jews in addition to the racially well-mixed American Negro. You have persons of every conceivable shade and color. Persons speaking all languages, persons representative of many cultures and civilizations. Harlem is a magic melting pot, a modern Babel mocking the gods with its cosmopolitan uniqueness.

The American Negro predominates and, having adopted all of white America's prejudices and manners, is inclined to look askance at his little dark-skinned brothers from across the sea. The Spanish Negro, i. e., those Negroes hailing from Spanish possessions, stays to himself and has little traffic with the other racial groups in his environment. The other foreigners, with the exception of the British West Indians are not large enough to form a separate social group and generally become quickly identified with the regulation social life of the community.

It is the Negro from the British West Indies who creates and has to face a disagreeable problem. Being the second largest Negro Group in Harlem, and being less susceptible to American manners and customs than others, he is frowned upon and berated by the American Negro. This intraracial prejudice is an amazing though natural thing. Imagine a community made up of people universally known as oppressed, wasting time and energy trying to oppress others of their kind, more recently transplanted from a foreign clime. It is easy to explain. All people seem subject to prejudice, even those who suffer from it most, and all people seem inherently to dislike other folk who are characterized by cultural and lingual differences. It is a failing of man, a curse of humanity, and if these differences are accompanied, as they usually are, by quarrels concerning economic matters, there is bound to be an intensifying of the bitter antagonism existent between the two groups. Such has been the case with the British West Indian in Harlem. Because of his numerical strength, because of his cockney English inflections and accent, because of his unwillingness to submit to certain American do's and don'ts, and because he, like most foreigners, has seemed willing to work for low wages, he has been hated and abused by his fellow-Harlemites. And, as a matter of protection, he has learned to fight back.

It has been said that West Indians are comparable to Jews in that they are "both ambitious, eager for education, willing to engage in business, argumentative, aggressive, and possess a great proselytizing zeal for any cause they espouse." Most of the retail business in Harlem is owned and controlled by West Indians. They are also well represented and often officiate as provocative agents and leaders in radical movements among Harlem Negroes. And it is obvious that the average American Negro, in manifesting a dislike for the West Indian Negro, is being victimized by that same delusion which he claims blinds the American white man; namely, that all Negroes are alike. There are some West Indians who are distasteful; there are some of all people about whom one could easily say the same thing.

It is to be seen then that all this widely diversified population would erect an elaborate social structure. For instance, there are thousands of Negroes in New York from Georgia. These have organized themselves into many clubs, such as the Georgia Circle or the Sons of Georgia. People from Virginia, South Carolina, Florida and other states do likewise. The foreign contingents also seem to have a mania for social organization.

Social clubs and secret lodges are legion. And all of them vie with one another in giving dances, parties, entertainments and benefits in addition to public turnouts and parades.

Speaking of parades, one must mention Marcus Garvey. Garvey, a Jamaican, is one of the most widely known Negroes in contemporary life. He became notorious because of his Back-to-Africa campaign. With the West Indian population of Harlem as a nucleus, he enlisted the aid of thousands of Negroes all over America in launching the Black Star Line, the purpose of which was to establish a trade and travel route between America and Africa by and for Negroes. He also planned to establish a black empire in Africa of which he was to be emperor. The man's imagination and influence were colossal; his manifestations of these qualities often ridiculous and adolescent, though they seldom lacked color and interest.

Garvey added much to the gaiety and life of Harlem with his parades. Garmented in a royal purple robe with crimson trimmings and an elaborate headdress, he would ride in state down Seventh Avenue in an open limousine, surrounded and followed by his personal cabinet of high chieftains, ladies in waiting and protective legion. Since his incarceration in Atlanta Federal prison on a charge of having used the mails to defraud, Harlem knows no more such spectacles. The street parades held now are uninteresting and pallid when compared to the Garvey turnouts, brilliantly primitive as they were.

In addition to the racial and territorial divisions of the social structure there are also minor divisions determined by color and wealth. First there are the "dictys," that class of Negroes who constitute themselves as the upper strata and have lately done much wailing in the public places because white and black writers have seemingly overlooked them in their delineations of Negro life in Harlem. This upper strata is composed of the more successful and more socially inclined professional folk—lawyers, doctors, dentists, druggists, politicians, beauty parlor proprietors and real estate dealers. They are for the most part mulattoes of light brown skin and have succeeded in absorbing all the social mannerisms of the white American middle class. They live in the stately rows of houses on 138th and 139th Streets between Seventh and Eighth Avenues or else in the "high-tone" apartment houses on Edgecombe and St. Nicholas. They are both stupid and snobbish as is their class in any race. Their most compelling if sometimes unconscious ambition is to be as near white as possible, and their greatest expenditure of energy is concentrated on eradicating any trait or characteristic commonly known as negroid.

Their homes are expensively appointed and comfortable. Most of them are furnished in good taste, thanks to the interior decorator who was hired to do the job. Their existence is one of smug complacence. They are well satisfied with themselves and with their class. They are without a doubt the basic element from which the Negro aristocracy of the future will evolve. They are also good illustrations, mentally, sartorially and socially, of what the American standardizing machine can do to susceptible material.

These people have a social life of their own. They attend formal dinners and dances, resplendent in chic expensive replicas of Fifth Avenue finery. They arrange suitable inter-coterie weddings, preside luxuriously at announcement dinners, pre-nuptial showers, wedding breakfasts and the like. They attend church socials, fraternity dances and sorority gatherings. They frequent the downtown theaters, and occasionally, quite occasionally, drop into one of the Harlem night clubs which certain of their lower caste brethren frequent and white downtown excursionists make wealthy.

Despite this upper strata which is quite small, social barriers among Negroes are not as strict and well regulated in Harlem as they are in other Negro communities. Like all cosmopolitan centers Harlem is democratic. People associate with all types should chance happen to throw them together. There are a few aristocrats, a plethora of striving bourgeoisie, a few artistic spirits and a great proletarian mass, which constitutes the most interesting and important element in Harlem, for it is this latter class and their institutions that gives the community its color and fascination.

IV
NIGHT LIFE IN HARLEM

Much has been written and said about night life in Harlem. It has become the *leit motif* of sophisticated conversation and shop girl intimacies. To call yourself a New Yorker you must have been to Harlem at least once. Every up-to-date person knows Harlem, and knowing Harlem generally means that one has visited a night club or two. These night clubs are now enjoying much publicity along with the New Negro and Negro art. They are the shrines to which white sophisticates, Greenwich Village artists, Broadway revellers and provincial commuters make eager pilgrimage. In fact, the white patronage is so profitable and so abundant that Negroes find themselves crowded out and even segregated in their own places of jazz.

There are, at the present time, about one dozen of these night clubs in Harlem—Bamville, Connie's Inn, Baron Wilkins, The Nest, Small's Paradise, The Capitol, The Cotton Club, The Green Cat, The Sugar Cane Club, Happy Rhones, The Hoofers Club and the Little Savoy. Most of these generally have from two to ten white persons for every black one. Only The Hoofers, The Little Savoy, and The Sugar Cane Club seem to cater almost exclusively to Negro trade.

At the Bamville and at Small's Paradise, one finds smart white patrons, the type that reads the ultrasophisticated *New Yorker*. Indeed, that journal says in its catalogue of places to go—"Small's and Bamville are the show places of Harlem for downtowners on their first excursion. Go late. Better not to dress." And so the younger generation of Broadway, Park Avenue, Riverside Drive, Third Avenue and the Bronx go late, take their own gin, applaud the raucous vulgarity of the entertainers, dance with abandon and go home with a headache. They have seen Harlem.

The Cotton Club and Connie's Inn make a bid for theatrical performers and well-to-do folk around town. The Nest and Happy Rhones attract traveling salesmen, store clerks and commuters from Jersey and Yonkers. The Green Cat has a large Latin clientele. Baron Wilkins draws glittering ladies from Broadway with their sleek gentlemen friends. Because of these conditions of invasion, Harlem's far-famed night clubs have become merely side shows staged for sensation-seeking whites. Nevertheless, they are still an egregious something to experience. Their smoking cavernous depths are eerie and ecstatic. Patrons enter, shiver involuntarily, then settle down to be shoved about and scared by the intangible rhythms that surge all around them. White night clubs are noisy. White night clubs affect weird music, soft light, Negro entertainers and dancing waiters, but, even with all these contributing elements, they cannot approximate the infectious rhythm and joy always found in a Negro cabaret.

Take the Sugar Cane Club on Fifth Avenue near 135th Street, located on the border of the most "low-down" section of Harlem. This place is visited by few whites or few "dicty" Negroes. Its customers are the rough-and-ready, happy-go-lucky more primitive type—street walkers, petty gamblers and pimps, with an occasional adventurer from other strata of society.

The Sugar Cane Club is a narrow subterranean passageway about twenty-five feet wide and 125 feet long. Rough wooden tables, surrounded by rough wooden chairs, and the orchestra stands, jammed into the right wall center, use up about three-quarters of the space. The remaining rectangular area is bared for dancing. With a capacity for seating about one hundred people, it usually finds room on gala nights for twice that many. The orchestra weeps and moans and groans as only an unsophisticated Negro jazz orchestra can. A blues singer croons vulgar ditties over the tables to individual parties or else wah-wahs husky syncopated blues songs from the center of the floor. Her act over, the white lights are extinguished, red and blue spot lights are centered on the diminutive dancing space, couples push back their chairs, squeeze out from behind the tables and from against the wall, then finding one another's bodies, sweat gloriously together, with shoulders hunched, limbs obscenely intertwined and hips wiggling; animal beings urged on by liquor and music and physical contact.

Small's Paradise, on Seventh Avenue near 135th Street, is just the opposite of the Sugar Cane Club. It caters almost exclusively to white trade with just enough Negroes present to give the necessary atmosphere and "difference." Yet even in Small's with its symphonic orchestra, full-dress appearance and dignified onlookers, there is a great deal of that unexplainable, intangible rhythmic presence so characteristic of a Negro cabaret.

In addition to the well-known cabarets, which are largely show places to curious whites, there are innumerable places—really speak-easies—which are open only to the initiate. These places are far more colorful and more full of spontaneous joy than the larger places to which one has ready access. They also furnish more thrills to the spectator. This is possible because the crowd is more select, the liquor more fiery, the atmosphere more intimate and the activities of the patrons not subject to be watched by open-mouthed white people from downtown and the Bronx.

One particular place known as the Glory Hole is hidden in a musty damp basement behind an express and trucking office. It is a single room about ten feet square and remains an unembellished basement except for a planed down plank floor, a piano, three chairs and a library table. The Glory Hole is typical of its class. It is a social club, commonly called a dive, convenient for the high times of a certain group. The men are unskilled laborers during the day, and in the evenings they round up their girls or else meet them at the rendezvous in order to have what they consider and enjoy as a good time. The women, like the men, swear, drink and dance as much and as vulgarly as they please. Yet they do not strike the observer as being vulgar. They are merely being and doing what their environment and their desire for pleasure suggest.

Such places as the Glory Hole can be found all over the so-called "bad lands" of Harlem. They are not always confined to basement rooms. They can be found in apartment flats, in the rear of barber shops, lunch counters, pool halls, and other such conveniently blind places. Each one has its regular quota of customers with just enough new patrons introduced from time to time to keep the place alive and prosperous. These intimate, low-down civic centers are occasionally misjudged. Social service reports damn them with the phrase "breeding places of vice and crime." They may be. They are also good training grounds for prospective pugilists. Fights are staged with regularity and with vigor. And most of the regular customers have some mark on their faces or bodies that can be displayed as having been received during a battle in one of the glory holes.

The other extreme of amusement places in Harlem is exemplified by the Bamboo Inn, a Chinese-American restaurant that features Oriental cuisine, a jazz band and dancing. It is the place for select Negro Harlem's night life, the place where debutantes have their coming out parties, where college lads take their co-eds and society sweethearts and where dignified matrons entertain. It is a beautifully decorated establishment, glorified by a balcony with booths, and a large gyroflector, suspending from the center of the ceiling, on which colored spotlights play, flecting the room with triangular bits of vari-colored light. The Bamboo Inn is *the* place to see "high Harlem," just like the Glory Hole is *the* place to see "low Harlem." Well-dressed men escorting expensively garbed women and girls; models from Vanity Fair with brown, yellow and black skins. Doctors and lawyers, Babbitts and their ladies with fine manners (not necessarily learned through Emily Post), fine clothes and fine homes to return to when the night's fun has ended.

The music plays. The gyroflector revolves. The well-bred, polite dancers mingle on the dance floor. There are a few silver hip flasks. There is an occasional burst of too-spontaneous-for-the-environment laughter. The Chinese waiters slip around, quiet and bored. A big black-face bouncer, arrayed in tuxedo, watches eagerly for some too boisterous, too unconventional person to put out. The Bamboo Inn has only one blemishing feature. It is also the rendezvous for a set of oriental men who favor white women, and who, with their pale face partners, mingle with Harlem's four hundred.

When Harlem people wish to dance, without attending a cabaret, they go to the Renaissance Casino or to the Savoy, Harlem's two most famous public dance halls. The Savoy is the pioneer in the field of giving dance-loving Harlemites some place to gather nightly. It is an elaborate ensemble with a Chinese garden (Negroes seem to have a penchant for Chinese food—there are innumerable Chinese restaurants all over Harlem), two orchestras that work in relays, and hostesses provided at twenty-five cents per dance for partnerless young men. The Savoy opens at three in the afternoon and closes at three in the morning. One can spend twelve hours in this jazz palace for sixty-five cents, and the price of a dinner or an occasional sustaining sandwich and drink. The music is good, the dancers are gay, and the setting is conducive to joy.

The Renaissance Casino was formerly a dance hall, rented out only for social affairs, but when the Savoy began to flourish, the Renaissance, after closing a while for redecorations, changed its policy and reopened as a public dance hall. It has no lounging room or Chinese garden, but it stages a basket ball game every Sunday night that is one of the most popular amusement institutions in Harlem, and it has an exceptionally good orchestra, comfortable sitting-out places and a packed dance floor nightly.

Then, when any social club wishes to give a dance at the Renaissance, the name of the organization is flashed from the electric signboard that hangs above the entrance and in return for the additional and assured crowd, some division of the door receipts is made. The Renaissance is, I believe, in good Harlemese, considered more "dicty" than the Savoy. It has a more regulated and more dignified clientele, and almost every night in the week the dances are sponsored by some well-known social group.

In addition to the above two places, the Manhattan Casino, an elaborate dance palace, is always available for the more de luxe gatherings. It is at the Manhattan Casino that the National Association for the Advancement of Colored People has its yearly whist tournament and dance, that Harlem society folk have their charity balls, and select formals, and that the notorious Hamilton Lodge holds its spectacular masquerade each year.

All of the dances held in this Casino are occasions never to be forgotten. Hundreds of well-dressed couples dancing on the floor. Hundreds of Negroes of all types and colors, mingling together on the dance floor, gathering in the boxes, meeting and conversing on the promenade. And here and there an occasional white person, or is it a Negro who can "pass"?

Negroes love to dance, and in Harlem where the struggle to live is so intensely complex, the dance serves as a welcome and feverish outlet. Yet it is strange that none of these dance palaces are owned or operated by Negroes. The Renaissance Casino was formerly owned by a syndicate of West Indians, but has now fallen into the hands of a Jewish group. And despite the thousands of dollars Negroes spend in order to dance, the only monetary returns in their own community are the salaries paid to the Negro musicians, ushers, janitors and door-men. The rest of the profits are spent and exploited outside of Harlem.

This is true of most Harlem establishments. The Negro in Harlem is not, like the Negro in Chicago and other metropolitan centers, in charge of the commercial enterprises located in his community. South State Street in Chicago's great Black belt, is studded with Negro banks, Negro office buildings, housing Negro insurance companies, manufacturing concerns, and other major enterprises. There are no Negro controlled banks in Harlem. There are only branches of downtown Manhattan's financial institutions, manned solely by whites and patronized almost exclusively by Negroes. Harlem has no outstanding manufacturing concern like the Overton enterprises in Chicago, the Poro school and factory in St. Louis, or the Madame Walker combine in Indianapolis. Harlem Negroes own over sixty million dollars worth of real estate, but they neither own nor operate one first-class grocery store, butchershop, dance hall, theater, clothing store or saloon. They do invest their money in barber shops, beauty parlors, pool halls, tailor shops, restaurants and lunch counters.

V
THE AMUSEMENT
LIFE OF HARLEM

Like most good American communities the movies hold a primary position in the amusement life of Harlem. There are seven neighborhood motion picture houses in Negro Harlem proper, and about six big time cinema palaces on 125th Street that have more white patronage than black, yet whose audiences are swelled by movie fans from downtown.

The picture emporiums of Harlem are comparable to those in any residential neighborhood. They present second and third run features with supporting bills of comedies, novelties, and an occasional special performance when the management presents a bathing beauties contest, a plantation jubilee, an amateur ensemble and other vaudeville stunts. The Renaissance Theater, in the same building with the Renaissance Casino, is the cream of Harlem motion picture houses. It, too, was formerly owned and operated by Negroes, the only one of its kind in Harlem. Now Negroes only operate it. The Renaissance attracts the more select movie audiences; it has a reputable symphony orchestra, a Wurlitzer organ, and presents straight movies without vaudeville flapdoodle. It is spacious and clean and free from disagreeable odors.

The Roosevelt Theater, the New Douglas, and the Savoy are less aristocratic competitors. They show the same pictures as the Renaissance, but seem to be patronized by an entirely different set of people, and, although their interiors are more spacious, they are not as well decorated or as clean as the Renaissance. They attract a set of fresh youngsters, smart aleck youths and lecherous adult males who attend, not so much to see the picture as to pick up a susceptible female or to spoon with some girl they have picked up elsewhere. The places are also frequented by family groups, poor but honest folk, who cannot afford other forms or places of amusement.

The Franklin and the Gem are the social outcasts of the group. Their audiences are composed almost entirely of loafers from the low-grade pool rooms and dives in their vicinity, and tenement-trained drudges from the slums. The stench in these two places is nauseating. The Board of Health rules are posted conspicuously, admonishing patrons not to spit on the floor or to smoke in the auditorium, but the aisle is slippery with tobacco spew and cigarette smoke adds to the density of the foul air. The movies flicker on the screen, some wild west picture three or four years old, dirty babies cry in time with the electric piano that furnishes the music, men talk out loud, smoke, spit, and drop empty gin or whiskey bottles on the floor when emptied.

All of these places from the Renaissance to the Gem are open daily from two in the afternoon until eleven at night, and save for a lean audience during the supper hour are usually filled to capacity. Saturdays, Sundays and holidays are harvest times, and the Jewish representatives of the chain to which a theater belongs walk around excitedly and are exceedingly gracious, thinking no doubt of the quarters that are being deposited at the box office.

The Lafayette and Lincoln theaters are three-a-day combination movie and musical comedy revue houses. The Lafayette used to house a local stock company composed of all Negro players, but it has now fallen into less dignified hands. Each week it presents a new revue. These revues are generally weak-kneed, watery variations on downtown productions. If Earl Carroll is presenting Artists and Models on Broadway, the Lafayette presents Brown Skin Models in Harlem soon afterwards. Week after week one sees same type of "high yaller" chorus, hears the same blues songs, and applauds different dancers doing the same dance steps. There is little originality on the part of the performers, and seldom any change of fare. Cheap imitations of Broadway successes, nudity, vulgar dances and vulgar jokes are the box office attractions.

On Friday nights there is a midnight show, which is one of the most interesting spectacles in Harlem. The performance begins some time after midnight and lasts until four or four-thirty the next morning. The audience is as much if not more interesting and amusing than the performers on the stage. Gin bottles are carried and passed among groups of friends. Cat calls and hisses attend any dull bit. Outspoken comments punctuate the lines, songs and dances of the performers. Impromptu acts are staged in the orchestra and in the gallery. The performers themselves are at their best and leave the stage to make the audience a part of their act. There are no conventions considered, no reserve is manifested. Everyone has a jolly good time, and after the theater there are parties or work according to the wealth and inclinations of the individual.

The Lincoln theater is smaller and more smelly than the Lafayette, and most people who attend the latter will turn up their noses at the Lincoln. It too has revues and movies, and its only distinguishing feature is that its shows are even worse than those staged at the Lafayette. They are so bad that they are ludicrously funny. The audience is comparable to that found in the Lafayette on Friday nights at the midnight jamboree. Performers are razzed. Chorus girls are openly courted or damned, and the spontaneous utterances of the patrons are far more funny than any joke the comedians ever tell. If one can stand the stench, one can have a good time for three hours or more just by watching the unpredictable and surprising reactions of the audience to what is being presented on the stage.

VI
HOUSE RENT PARTIES, NUMBERS AND HOT MEN

The Harlem institutions that intrigue the imagination and stimulate the most interest on the part of an investigator are House Rent Parties, Numbers and Hot Men. House Rent parties are the result of high rents. Private houses containing nine or ten or twelve rooms rent from $185 up to $250 per month. Apartments are rated at $20 per room or more, according to the newness of the building and the conveniences therein. Five-room flats, located in walk-up tenements, with inside rooms, dark hallways and dirty stairs rent for $10 per room or more. It can be seen then that when the average Negro workingman's salary is considered (he is often paid less for his labors than a white man engaged in the same sort of work), and when it is also considered that he and his family must eat, dress and have some amusements and petty luxuries, these rents assume a criminal enormity. And even though every available bit of unused space is sublet at exorbitant rates to roomers, some other source of revenue is needed when the time comes to meet the landlord.

Hence we have hundreds of people opening their apartments and houses to the public, their only stipulation being that the public pay twenty-five cents admission fee and buy plentifully of the food and drinks offered for sale. Although one of these parties can be found any time during the week, Saturday night is favored. The reasons are obvious; folk don't have to get up early on Sunday morning and most of them have had a pay day.

Of course, this commercialization of spontaneous pleasure in order to pay the landlord has been abused, and now there are folk who make their living altogether by giving alleged House Rent Parties. This is possible because there are in Harlem thousands of people with no place to go, thousands of people lonesome, unattached and cramped, who stroll the streets eager for a chance to form momentary contacts, to dance, to drink and make merry. They willingly part with more of the week's pay than they should just to enjoy an oasis in the desert of their existence and a joyful intimate party, open to the public yet held in a private home, is, as they say, "their meat."

So elaborate has the technique of these parties and their promotion become that great competition has sprung up between prospective party givers. Private advertising stunts are resorted to, and done quietly so as not to attract too much attention from the police, who might want to collect a license fee or else drop in and search for liquor. Cards are passed out in pool halls, subway stations, cigar stores, and on the street. This is an example:

> Hey! Hey!
> Come on boys and girls let's shake
> that thing
> Where?
> At
> Hot Poppa Sam's
> West 134th Street, three flights up.
> Jelly Roll Smith at the piano
> Saturday night, May 7, 1927
> Hey! Hey!

Saturday night comes. There may be only piano music, there may be a piano and drum, or a three or four-piece ensemble. Red lights, dim and suggestive, are in order. The parlor and the dining room are cleared for the dance, and one bedroom is utilized for hats and coats. In the kitchen will be found boiled pigs feet, ham hock and cabbage, hopping John (a combination of peas and rice), and other proletarian dishes.

The music will be barbarous and slow. The dancers will use their bodies and the bodies of their partners without regard to the conventions. There will be little restraint. Happy individuals will do solo specialties, will sing, dance—have Charleston and Black Bottom contests and break-downs. Hard little tenement girls will flirt and make dates with Pool Hall Johnnies and drug store cowboys. Prostitutes will drop in and slink out. And in addition to the liquor sold by the house, flasks of gin, and corn and rye will be passed around and emptied. Here "low" Harlem is in its glory, primitive and unashamed.

I have counted as many as twelve such parties in one block, five in one apartment house containing forty flats. They are held all over Harlem with the possible exception of 137th, 138th and 139th Streets between Seventh and Eighth Avenues where the bulk of Harlem's upper class lives. Yet the house rent party is not on the whole a vicious institution. It serves a real and vital purpose, and is as essential to "low Harlem" as the cultured receptions and soirees held on "strivers' row" are to "high Harlem."

House rent parties have their evils; it is an economic evil and a social evil that makes them necessary, but they also have their virtues. Like all other institutions of man it depends upon what perspective you view them from. But regardless of abstract matters, house rent parties do provide a source of revenue to those in difficult financial straits, and they also give lonesome Harlemites, caged in by intangible bars, some place to have their fun and forget problems of color, civilization and economics.

Numbers, unlike house rent parties, is not an institution confined to any one class of Harlem folk. Almost everybody plays the numbers, a universal and illegal gambling pastime, which has become Harlem's favorite indoor sport.

Numbers is one of the most elaborate, big-scale lottery games in America. It is based on the digits listed in the daily reports of the New York stock exchange. A person wishing to play the game places a certain sum of money, from one penny up, on a number composed of three digits. This number must be placed in the hands of a runner before ten o'clock in the morning as the reports are printed in the early editions of the afternoon papers. The clearing house reports are like this:

Exchanges	$1,023,000,000
Balances	128,000,000
Credit Bal.	98,000,000

The winning number is composed from the second and third digits in the millionth figures opposite exchanges and from the third figure in the millionth place opposite the balances. Thus if the report is like the example above, the winning number for that day will be 238.

An elaborate system of placement and paying off has grown around this game. Hundreds of persons known as runners make their rounds daily, collecting number slips and cash placements from their clients. These runners are the middle men between the public and the banker, who pays the runner a commission on all collections, reimburses winners, if there are any, and also gives the runner a percentage of his client's winnings.

These bankers and runners can well afford to be and often are rogues. Since numbers is an illegal pastime, they can easily disappear when the receipts are heavy or a number of people have chosen the correct three digits and wish their winnings. The police are supposed to make some effort to enforce the law and check the game. Occasionally a runner or a banker is arrested, but this generally occurs only when some irate player notifies the police that he "aint been done right by." Numbers can be placed in innumerable ways, the grocer, the butcher, the confectioner, the waitress at the lunch counter, the soda clerk, and the choir leader all collect slips for the number bankers.

People look everywhere for a number to play. The postman passes, some addict notes the number on his cap and puts ten cents on it for that day. A hymn is announced by the pastor in church and all the members in the congregation will note the number for future reference. People dream, each dream is a symbol for a number that can be ascertained by looking in a dream book for sale at all Harlem newsstands. Street car numbers, house numbers, street numbers, chance calculations—anything that has figures on it or connected with it will give some player a good number, and inspire him to place much money on it.

There is slight chance to win, it is a thousand to one shot, and yet this game and its possible awards have such a hold on the community that it is often the cause for divorce, murder, scanty meals, dispossess notices and other misfortunes. Some player makes a "hit" for one dollar, and receives five hundred and forty dollars. Immediately his acquaintances and neighbors are in a frenzy and begin staking large sums on any number their winning friend happens to suggest.

It is all a game of chance. There is no way to figure out scientifically or otherwise what digits will be listed in the clearing house reports. Few people placing fifty cents on No. 238 stop to realize now many other combinations of three digits are liable to win. One can become familiar with the market's slump days and fat days, but even then the digits which determine the winning number could be almost anything.

People who are moral in every other respect, church going folk, who damn drinking, dancing, or gambling in any other form, will play the numbers. For some vague reason this game is not considered as gambling, and its illegality gives little concern to any one—even to the Harlem police, who can be seen slipping into a corner cigar store to place their number for the day with an obliging and secretive clerk.

As I write a friend of mine comes in with a big roll of money, $540. He has made a "hit." I guess I will play fifty cents on the number I found stamped inside the band of my last year's straw hat.

Stroll down Seventh Avenue on a spring Sunday afternoon. Everybody seems to be well dressed. The latest fashions prevail, and though there are the usual number of folk attired in outlandish color combinations and queer styles, the majority of the promenaders are dressed in good taste. In the winter, expensive fur coats swathe the women of Harlem's Seventh Avenue as they swathe the pale face fashionplates on Fifth Avenue down town, while the men escorting them are usually sartorially perfect.

How is all this well-ordered finery possible? Most of these people are employed as menials—dish washers, elevator operators, porters, waiters, red caps, longshoremen, and factory hands. Their salaries are notoriously low, not many men picked at random on Seventh Avenue can truthfully say that they regularly earn more than $100 per month, and from this salary must come room rent, food and other of life's necessities and luxuries. How can they dress so well?

There are, of course, the installment houses, considered by many authorities one of the main economic curses of our present day civilization, and there are numerous people who run accounts at such places just to keep up a front, but these folk have little money to jingle in their pockets. All of it must be dribbled out to the installment collectors. There was even one chap I knew, who had to pawn a suit he had bought on the installment plan in order to make the final ten dollar payment and prevent the credit house collector from garnisheeing his wages. And it will be found that the majority of the Harlemites, who must dress well on a small salary, shun the installment house leechers and patronize the "hot men."

"Hot men" sell "hot stuff," which when translated from Harlemese into English, means merchandise supposedly obtained illegally and sold on the q. t. far below par. "Hot men" do a big business in Harlem. Some have apartments fitted out as showrooms, but the majority peddle their goods piece by piece from person to person.

"Hot stuff" is supposedly stolen by shoplifters or by store employes or by organized gangs, who raid warehouses and freight yards. Actually, most of the "hot stuff" sold in Harlem originally comes from bankrupt stores. Some ingenious group of people make a practice of attending bankruptcy sales and by buying blocks of merchandise get a great deal for a small sum of money. This merchandise is then given in small lots to various agents in Harlem, who secretly dispose of it.

There is a certain glamour about buying stolen goods aside from their cheapness. Realizing this, "hot men" and their agents maintain that their goods are stolen whether they are or not. People like to feel that they are breaking the law and when they are getting undeniable bargains at the same time, the temptation becomes twofold. Of course, one never really knows whether what they are buying has been stolen from a neighbor next door or bought from a defunct merchant. There have been many instances when a gentleman, strolling down the avenue in a newly acquired overcoat, has had it recognized by a former owner, and found himself either beaten up or behind the bars. However, such happenings are rare, for the experienced Harlemite will buy only that "hot stuff" which is obviously not second-hand.

One evening I happened to be sitting in one of the private reception rooms of the Harlem Y. W. C. A. There was a great commotion in the adjoining room, a great coming in and going out. It seemed as if every girl in the Y. W. C. A. was trying to crowd into that little room. Finally the young lady I was visiting went to investigate. She was gone for about fifteen minutes. When she returned she had on a new hat, which she informed me, between laughs at the bewildered expressions on my face, she had obtained from a "hot man" for two dollars. This same hat, according to her, would cost $10 downtown and $12 on 125th Street.

I placed my chair near the door and watched the procession of young women entering the room bareheaded and leaving with new head gear. Finally the supply was exhausted and a perspiring little Jew emerged, his pockets filled with dollar bills. I discovered later that this man was a store keeper in Harlem, who had picked up a large supply of spring hats at a bankruptcy sale and stating that it was "hot stuff" had proceeded to sell it not openly in his store, but sub rosa in private places.

There is no limit to the "hot man's" supply or the variety of goods he offers. One can, if one knows the ropes, buy any article of wearing apparel from him. And in addition to the professional "hot man" there are always the shoplifters and thieving store clerks, who accost you secretly and eagerly place at your disposal what they have stolen.

Hence low salaried folk in Harlem dress well, and Seventh Avenue is a fashionable street crowded with expensively dressed people, parading around in all their "hot" finery. A cartoonist in a recent issue of one of the Negro monthlies depicted the following scene: A number of people at a fashionable dance are informed that the police have come to search for some individual known to be wearing stolen goods. Immediately there is a confused and hurried exodus from the room because all of the dancers present were arrayed in "hot stuff."

This, of course, is exaggerated. There are thousands of well-dressed people in Harlem able to be well-dressed not because they patronize a "hot man," but because their incomes make it possible. But there are a mass of people, working for small wages, who make good use of the "hot man," for not only can they buy their much wanted finery cheaply, but, thanks to the obliging "hot man," can buy it on the installment plan. Under the circumstances, who cares about breaking the law?

VII
THE NEGRO AND
THE CHURCH

The Negro in America has always supported his religious institutions even though he would not support his schools or business enterprises. Migrating to the city has not lessened his devotion to religious institutions even if it has lessened his religious fervor. He still donates a portion of his income to the church, and the church is still a major social center in all Negro communities.

Harlem is no exception to this rule, and its finest buildings are the churches. Their attendance is large, their prosperity amazing. Baptist, Methodist, Episcopal, Catholic, Presbyterian, Seventh Day Adventist, Spiritualist, Holy Roller and Abyssinian Jew—every sect and every creed with all their innumerable subdivisions can be found in Harlem.

The Baptist and the Methodist churches have the largest membership. There are more than a score of each. St. Phillips Episcopal Church is the most wealthy as well as one of the oldest Negro churches in New York. It owns a great deal of Harlem real estate and was one of the leading factors in urging Negroes to buy property in Harlem.

There are few new church buildings, most of them having been bought from white congregations when the Negro invaded Harlem and claimed it for his own. The most notable of the second-hand churches are the Metropolitan Baptist Church at 128th Street and Seventh Avenue, Salem M. E. Church at 129th Street and Seventh Avenue, and Mt. Olive Baptist Church at 120th Street and Lenox Avenue. This latter church has had a varied career. It was first a synagogue, then it was sold to white Seventh Day Adventists and finally fell into its present hands.

The most notable new churches are the Abyssinian Baptist Church on 138th Street, Mother Zion on 137th Street, and St. Marks. The latter church has just recently been finished. It is a dignified and colossal structure occupying a triangular block on Edgecombe and St. Nicholas Avenues between 137th and 138th Streets. It is the latest thing in churches, with many modern attachments—gymnasium, swimming pool, club rooms, Sunday school quarters, and other sub-auditoriums. When it was formally opened there was a gala dedication week to celebrate the occasion. Each night services were held by the various secret societies, the Elks, the Masons, the Knights of Pythias, the Odd Fellows, and others. The members of every local chapter of the various orders turned out to do homage to the new edifice. The collection proceeds were donated to the church.

St. Marks goes in for elaborate ceremony quite reminiscent of the Episcopal or Roman Catholic service. The choir is regaled in flowing robes and chants hymns by Handel. The pulpit is a triumph of carving and wood decoration. There is more ceremony than sermon.

The better class of Harlemites attends the larger churches. Most of the so-called "dictys" are registered as "Episcopalians" at St. Phillips, which is the religious sanctum of the socially elect and wealthy Negroes of Harlem. The congregation at St. Phillips is largely mulatto. This church has a Parish House that serves as one of the most ambitious and important social centers in Harlem. It supports a gymnasium that produces annually a first-class basket ball team, an art sketch class that is both large and promising, and other activities of interest and benefit to the community.

Every Sunday all of the churches are packed, and were they run entirely on the theatrical plan they would hang out the S. R. O. sign. No matter how large they are they do not seem to be large enough. And in addition to these large denominational churches there are many smaller ones also crowded, and a plethora of outlaw sects, ranging from Holy Rollers to Black Jews and Moslems.

The Holy Rollers collect in small groups of from twenty-five to one hundred and call themselves various things. Some are known as the Saints of God in Christ, others call themselves members of the Church of God and still others call themselves Sanctified Children of the Holy Ghost. Their meetings are primitive performances. Their songs and chants are lashing to the emotions. They also practice healing, and, during the course of their services, shout and dance as erotically and sincerely as savages around a jungle fire.

The Black Jews are a sect migrated from Abyssinia. Their services are similar to those in a Jewish Synagogue only they are of a lower order, for these people still believe in alchemy and practice polygamy when they can get away with it. Just recently a group of them were apprehended by agents from the Department of Justice for establishing a free love farm in the State of New Jersey. They were all citizens of Harlem and had induced many young Negro girls to join them.

The Mohammedans are beginning to send missionaries to work among Negroes in America. Already they have succeeded in getting enough converts in Harlem, Chicago, St. Louis and Detroit to establish mosques in these cities. There are about one hundred and twenty-five active members of the Mohammedan church in Harlem, practicing the precepts of the Koran under the leadership of an Islamic missionary.

The Spiritualist churches also thrive in Harlem. There are about twenty-five or more of their little chapels scattered about. They enjoy an enormous patronage from the more superstitious, ignorant classes. The leaders of the larger ones make most of their money from white clients, who drop in regularly for private sessions.

VIII
NEGRO JOURNALISM
IN HARLEM

The Harlem Negro owns, publishes, and supports five local weekly newspapers. These papers are just beginning to influence Harlem thought and opinion. For a long time they were merely purveyors of local gossip and scandal. Now some of them actually have begun to support certain issues for the benefit of the community and to cry out for reforms in the regulation journalistic manner.

For instance, *The New York Age*, which is the oldest Negro weekly in New York, has been conducting a publicity campaign against numbers and saloons. These saloons are to this paper as unwelcome a Harlem institution as the numbers. Each block along the main streets has at least one saloon, maybe two or three. They are open affairs, save instead of calling themselves saloons, they call themselves cafes. To get in is an easy matter. One has only to approach the door and look at a man seated on a box behind the front window, who acknowledges your look by pulling a chain which releases a bolt on the door. Once in you order what you wish from an old fashioned bartender and stand before an old-fashioned bar with a brass rail, mirrors, pictures, spittoons, and everything. What is more, they even have ladies' rooms in the rear.

The editor of *The New York Age*, in the process of conducting his crusade, published the addresses of all these saloons and urged that they be closed. The result of his campaign was that they are still open and doing more business than ever, thanks to his having informed people where they were located.

At first glance any of the Harlem newspapers give one the impression that Harlem is a hotbed of vice and crime. They smack of the tabloid in this respect and should be considered accordingly. True, there is vice and crime in Harlem as there is in any community where living conditions are chaotic and crowded.

For instance, there are 110 Negro women in Harlem for every 100 Negro men. Sixty and six-tenths percent of them are regularly employed. This, according to social service reports, makes women cheap, and conversely I suppose makes men expensive. Anyway there are a great number of youths and men who are either wholly or partially supported by single or married women. These male parasites, known as sweetbacks, dress well and spend their days standing on street corners, playing pool, gambling and looking for some other "fish" to aid in their support. This is considered by some an alarming condition inasmuch as many immigrant youths from foreign countries and rural southern American districts naturally inclined to be lazy, think that it is smart and citified to be a parasite and do almost anything in order to live without working.

The newspapers of Harlem seldom speak of this condition, but their headlines give eloquent testimony to the results, with their reports of gun play, divorce actions (and in New York State there is only one ground for divorce) and brick-throwing parties. These conditions are magnified, of course, by proximity, and really are not important at all when the whole vice and crime situation in greater New York is taken under consideration.

To return to the newspapers, *The Negro World* is the official organ of the Garvey Movement. At one time it was one of the most forceful weeklies among Negroes. Now it has little life or power; its life-giving mentor, Marcus Garvey, being in Atlanta Federal Prison. Its only interesting feature is the weekly manifesto Garvey issues from his prison sanctum, urging his followers to remain faithful to the cause and not fight among themselves while he is kept away from them.

The Amsterdam News is the largest and most progressive Negro weekly published in Harlem. It, like all of its contemporaries, is conservative in politics and policy, but it does feature the work of many of the leading Negro journalists and has the most forceful editorial page of the group, even if it does believe that most of the younger Negro artists are "bad New Negroes."

The New York News is a political sheet, affecting the tabloid form. *The Tattler* is a scandal sheet. It specializes in personalities and theatrical and sport news.

IX
THE NEW NEGRO

H arlem has been called the center of the American Negroes' cultural renaissance and the mecca of the New Negro. If this is so, it is so only because Harlem is a part of New York, the cultural and literary capital of America. And Harlem becomes the mecca of the so-called New Negro only because he imagines that once there he can enjoy the cultural contact and intellectual stimulation necessary for his growth.

This includes the young Negro writer who comes to Harlem in order to be near both patrons and publishers of literature, and the young Negro artist and musician who comes to Harlem in order to be near the most reputable artistic and musical institutions in the country.

These folk, along with the librarians employed at the Harlem Branch of the New York Public Library, a few of the younger, more cultured professional men and women and the school teachers, who can be found in the grammar and high schools all over the city, constitute the Negro intelligentsia. This group is sophisticated and small and more a part of New York's life than of Harlem's. Its members are accepted as social and intellectual equals among whites downtown, and can be found at informal and formal gatherings in any of the five boroughs that compose greater New York. Harlem to most of them is just a place of residence; they are not "fixed" there as are the majority of Harlem's inhabitants.

Then there are the college youngsters and local intellectuals, whose prototypes can be found in any community. These people plan to attend lectures and concerts, given under the auspices of the Y. M. C. A., Y. W. C. A., churches, and public school civic centers. They are the people who form intercollegiate societies, who stage fraternity go-to-school campaigns, who attend the course of lectures presented by the Harlem Branch of the New York Public Library, during the winter months, and who frequent the many musical and literary entertainments given by local talent in Harlem auditoriums.

Harlem is crowded with such folk. The three great major educational institutions of New York, Columbia, New York University and the College of the City of New York, have a large Negro student attendance. Then there are many never-will-be-top-notch literary, artistic and intellectual strivers in Harlem as there are all over New York. Since the well advertised "literary renaissance," it is almost a Negro Greenwich Village in this respect. Every other person one meets is writing a novel, a poem or a drama. And there is seemingly no end to artists who do oils, pianists who pound out Rachmaninoff's Prelude in C Sharp Minor, and singers, with long faces and rolling eyes, who sing spirituals.

X
HARLEM—MECCA OF THE NEW NEGRO

arlem, the so-called citadel of Negro achievement in the New World, the alleged mecca of the New Negro and the advertised center of colored America's cultural renaissance. Harlem, a thriving black city, pulsing with vivid passions, alive with colorful personalities, and packed with many types and classes of people.

Harlem is a dream city pregnant with wide-awake realities. It is a masterpiece of contradictory elements and surprising types. There is no end to its versatile presentation of people, personalities and institutions. It is a mad medley.

There seems to be no end to its numerical and geographical growth. It is spreading north, east, south and west. It is slowly pushing beyond the barriers imposed by white people. It is slowly uprooting them from their present homes in the near vicinity of Negro Harlem as it has uprooted them before. There must be expansion and Negro Harlem is too much a part of New York to remain sluggish and still while all around is activity and expansion. As New York grows, so will Harlem grow. As Negro America progresses, so will Negro Harlem progress.

New York is now most liberal. There is little racial conflict, and there have been no inter-racial riots since the San Juan Hill days. The question is will the relations between New York Negro and New York white man always remain as tranquil as they are today? No one knows, and once in Harlem one seldom cares, for the sight of Harlem gives any Negro a feeling of great security. It is too large and too complex to seem to be affected in any way by such a futile thing as race prejudice.

There is no typical Harlem Negro as there is no typical American Negro. There are too many different types and classes. White, yellow, brown and black and all the intervening shades. North American, South American, African and Asian; Northerner and Southerner; high and low; seer and fool—Harlem holds them all, and strives to become a homogeneous community despite its motley hodge-podge of incompatible elements, and its self-nurtured or outwardly imposed limitations.

www.ingramcontent.com/pod-product-compliance
Lightning Source LLC
Chambersburg PA
CBHW071435040426
42445CB00012BA/1366